EMBRACING AN ADULT FAITH

Marcus Borg
on What It Means to Be Christian

A 5-Session Study by Marcus Borg with Tim Scorer

Morehouse Education Resources,
a division of Church Publishing Incorporated
Editorial Offices: 600 Grant Street, Suite 400, Denver, CO 80203

For catalogs and orders call:
1-800-242-1918,
www.morehouseeducation.org

ISBN-13: 978-1-60674-057-6

TABLE OF CONTENTS

QUICK GUIDE TO THIS HANDBOOK

TEN things to know as you begin to work with this resource:

1. HANDBOOK + WORKBOOK

This handbook is a guide to the group process as well as a workbook for everyone in the group.

2. A FIVE-SESSION RESOURCE

This resource presents five distinct topics for study: *GOD – JESUS – SALVATION – PRACTICE – COMMUNITY.*

3. DVD-BASED RESOURCE

The teaching content in each session comes in the form of up to 10 minutes of input by Marcus Borg and 12 minutes of response by Borg and members of a small group.

4. EVERYONE GETS EVERYTHING

The handbook addresses everyone in the group, not one group leader. There is no separate "Leader's Guide."

5. GROUP FACILITATION

We based this resource on the understanding that someone will be designated as group facilitator for each session. You may choose the same person or a different person for each of the five sessions.

6. TIME FLEXIBILITY

Each of the five sessions is flexible and can be between one hour and two or more hours in length.

7. BUILD YOUR OWN SESSION

Each of the five sessions offers you four to seven OPTIONS for building your own session.

8. A FORMAT WITHIN EACH OPTION

Each of the options has three consistent elements: *Beginning Conversation, The Teaching* and *Group Response to the Teaching.*

9. BEFORE THE SESSION

Each session opens with five questions for participants to consider as preparation for the session.

10. CLOSING OPTION

For each session there is an option presenting a way of closing that emerges naturally from the content of the session.

BEYOND THE "QUICK GUIDE"

Helpful information and guidance for anyone using this resource:

1. HANDBOOK + WORKBOOK

This handbook is a guide to the group process as well as a workbook for everyone in the group.

- We hope the handbook gives you all the information you need to feel confident in shaping the program to work for you and your fellow group members.
- The work space provided in the handbook encourages you...
  — to respond to leading questions.
  — to write or draw your own reflections.
  — to note the helpful responses of other group members.

2. FIVE-SESSION RESOURCE

This resource presents five distinct topics for study: *GOD – JESUS – SALVATION – PRACTICE – COMMUNITY.*

- For this resource we selected five key faith issues for small groups to engage and explore that concern 21st-century Christians.
- Although there are places of overlap between the five topics, we presented each one as distinctively as possible. We hope that, by the end of the five sessions, you find an opportunity to engage the questions of faith that are most pressing for you today.

3. DVD-BASED RESOURCE

The teaching content in each session comes in the form of up to 10 minutes of input by Marcus Borg and 12 minutes of response by Borg and members of a small group.

- In no more than 10 minutes, Borg stimulates thoughtful and heartfelt conversation among his listeners.
- These edited conversations present group sharing that builds on Borg's initial teaching. We intend to present to you a model of small group interaction that is personal, respectful and engaged.
- You will notice that the participants in the DVD group also become our teachers. In a number of cases, quotes from the group members enrich the teaching component of this resource. This will also happen in your group; you will become teachers for one another.
- We hope that the DVD presentations spark conversations about those things that matter most to those who are walking the way of Jesus in the 21st century.

4. EVERYONE GETS EVERYTHING

The handbook addresses everyone in the group, not one group leader. There is no separate "Leader's Guide."

- Unlike many small group resources, this one makes no distinction between material for the group facilitator and for the participants. Everyone has it all!
- We believe this empowers you and your fellow group members to share creatively in the leadership.

5. GROUP FACILITATION

We designed this for you to designate a group facilitator for each session. It does not have to be the same person for all five sessions, because everyone has all the material. It is, however, essential that you and the other group members are clear about who is facilitating each session. One or two people still have to be responsible for these kind of things:

- making arrangements for the meeting space (see notes on Meeting Space, p. 9)
- setting up the space to be conducive to conversations about the things that matter most
- creating and leading an opening to the session (see notes on Opening, p. 9)
- helping the group decide on which options to focus on in that session
- facilitating the group conversation for that session
- keeping track of the time
- calling the group members to attend to the standards established for the group life (see notes on Group Standards, p. 9)
- creating space in the conversation for all to participate

- keeping the conversation moving along so that the group covers all that it set out to do
- ensuring that time is taken for a satisfying closing to the session
- making sure that everyone is clear about date, location and focus for the next session
- following up with people who missed the session

6. TIME FLEXIBILITY

Each of the five sessions is flexible and can be between one hour and two or more hours in length.

- We designed this resource for your group to tailor it to fit the space available in the life of the congregation or community using it. That might be Sunday morning for an hour before or after worship, two hours on a weekday evening, or 90 minutes on a weekday morning.
- Some groups might decide to spend two sessions on one topic. There's enough material in each of the five topics to do that. Rushing to get through more than the time comfortably allows results in people not having the opportunity to speak about the things that matter most, and that sometimes takes longer to get to.

7. BUILD YOUR OWN SESSION

Each of the five sessions offers you from four to seven OPTIONS for building your own session. How will you decide what options to use?

- One or two people might take on the responsibility of shaping the session based on what they think will appeal to the group members. This responsibility could be shared from week to week.
- The group might take time at the end of one session to look ahead and decide on the options they will cover in the next session. This could be time consuming.
- You might decide to do your personal preparation for the session (responding to the five questions), and when everyone comes together for the session, proceed on the basis of what topics interested people the most.

8. A FORMAT WITHIN EACH OPTION

Each of the options has three consistent elements: *Beginning Conversation, The Teaching* and *Group Response to the Teaching.*

- *Beginning Conversation* provides an opportunity for people to think about the topic prior to seeing the DVD presentation. This "tilling of the soil" prior to the planting of seeds of learning creates in learners a deeper readiness for new ideas. It also makes it more likely that this new information will be connected to the body of knowledge that the learner already brings.
- *The Teaching* offers the new input from the DVD. Sometimes it requires the group to watch the whole DVD presentation for that session; other times it asks the group to watch just the Borg presentation prior to watching the group conversation that follows Borg. For learners who are more visual than auditory, excerpts of the DVD recording sometimes appear as text.
- *Group Response to the Teaching* provides experiential material for the group to follow after viewing the DVD, a part of it, or printed statements from the DVD. This is a time when the members of the group work with the teaching and have the opportunity to integrate it into their own experience and frames of reference.

9. BEFORE THE SESSION

Each session opens with five questions for participants to consider as preparation for the session.

- We intend these questions to open in you some aspect of the topic being considered in the upcoming session. This may lead you to feel more confident when addressing this question in the group.
- Sometimes these questions are the same as ones raised in the context of the session. They provide opportunity for people to do some personal reflection prior to engaging in group conversation on that topic.

10. CLOSING OPTION

For each session there is a final option presenting a way of closing the session that emerges naturally from its content.

- It's important to close well. It's like a period at the end of a sentence. People leave the session ready for whatever comes next.
- Whether you use the closing option suggested or one of your own choosing, closing well matters.
- Another aspect of closing is evaluation. This is not included in an intentional way in the design of the sessions; however, evaluation is such a natural and satisfying thing to do that it could be included as part of the discipline of closing each session. It's as simple as taking time to respond to these questions:
  - What insights am I taking from this session?
  - What contributed to my learning?
  - What will I do differently as a result of my being here today?

POINTERS ON FACILITATION

1. Meeting Space

- Take time to prepare the space for the group. When people come into a space that has been prepared for them, they trust the hospitality, resulting in a willingness to bring the fullness of themselves into the conversation. Something as simple as playing recorded music as people arrive will contribute to this sense of "a space prepared for you."
- Think about how the space will encourage a spirit of reverence, intimacy and care. Will there be a table in the center of the circle where a candle can be lit each time the group meets? Is there room for other symbols that emerge from the group's life?

2. Opening

- In the opening session, take time to go around the circle and introduce yourselves in some way.
- Every time a group comes together again, it takes each member time to feel fully included. Some take longer than others. An important function of facilitation is to help this happen with ease, so people find themselves participating fully in the conversation as soon as possible. We designed these sessions with this in mind. Encouraging people to share in the activity proposed under *Beginning Conversation* is one way of supporting that feeling of inclusion.
- The ritual of opening might include the lighting of a candle, an opening prayer, the singing of a hymn where appropriate, and the naming of each person present.

3. Group Standards

- There are basic standards in group life that are helpful to name when a new group begins. Once they are named, you can always come back to them as a point of reference if necessary. Here are two basics:
  — Everything that is said in this group remains in the group. (confidentiality)
  — We will begin and end at the time agreed. (punctuality)
- Are there any others that you need to name as you begin? Sometimes standards emerge from the life of the group that need to be named at that time.

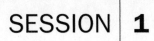

SESSION | 1

GOD

BEFORE THE SESSION

Many participants like to come to the group conversation after considering individually some of the issues that will be raised. The following five reflective questions are intended to open your minds, memories and emotions regarding some aspects of this session's topic. Use the space provided here to note your reflections.

What is your experience of God this week?

What words best help you express the reality of God in your life?

In what ways have you experienced and understood God at various stages of your life?

What riches grow out of your relationship with God at this time in your life?

What hymns, prayers and other writings express most accurately your experience of God?

OPTION 1: THE MEANING OF THE WORD GOD

Beginning Conversation

Say aloud words that you associate with the word *God*.

Note these on the newsprint page so that everyone can see them and reference them as needed.

Having heard all the words, use the space below to note the ones that have the most meaning for your group.

The Teaching

Play the first part of the DVD in which Borg asks the question, "What is the referent of the word *God*?"

Borg presents two responses to the question:
- the God of supernatural theism
  - a person-like being separate from the universe
  - an all-powerful, all-knowing, law-giving authority figure who loves us, but who may also punish us
  - one who occasionally intervenes in human affairs
- an encompassing reality or Spirit
  - the One in whom we live and move and have our being
  - the One in whom we live, as a fish lives in water
  - the reality of all that is
  - the One of whom mystics speak; "…a luminous light shining through everything…a falling away of sharp boundaries between ourselves and the world that marks our everyday consciousness…a place of amazement, wonder and joy in which I see more clearly than ever…"

Group Response to the Teaching

Like Borg, most people have known both of these meanings of the word *God*. Where are you now with regard to these two contrasting ways of thinking of God?

OPTION 2: WHAT GOD IS LIKE

Beginning Conversation

Say aloud the words and phrases that convey the nature (character and passion) of God to you. Note these on newsprint for future reference. Use the space below to note the words and phrases that carry the most meaning for you.

The Teaching

On the DVD Borg also addresses the question of what God is like. "What is God's character and passion?" he asks.

Consistent with the first part of his teaching, he presents God's nature in two ways:
- a God who is punitive and who might punish a sinner forever in hell—resulting in a relationship that includes fear
- a God who is gracious, compassionate and understood as an expression of the lines from John's gospel, "For God so loved the world…"—resulting in a relationship free of fear and full of awe

Group Response to the Teaching

To what extent have you experienced these two "God" realities?

What difference does the way someone sees God's character (1 or 2) make to his or her day-to-day living?

OPTION 3: SPEAKING OF GOD

Play the responses of the people who are in Borg's small group.

What a diversity of responses to Borg's teaching! Respond off the cuff to what you heard:

- Where did you find one of the DVD group members speaking for you?
- What issues were raised that concern you?
- Where did you find yourself wanting to respond in any way to someone on the recording?
- What questions are "live" for you in relation to this overall topic: God?

Some of these issues and questions may be addressed in the remaining options. Some you may have to answer in general conversation time or in one-to-one conversations.

OPTION 4: EXPERIENCING THE SACRED

Beginning Conversation

Share specific ways that you have experienced the reality of the sacred.

The Teaching

Borg says:

I come to this understanding (of God), not through intellectual effort, but through a series of experiences in my early thirties that I now recognize as mystical experiences. That's simply a way of saying experiences in which I saw whatever I was looking at—the same landscape or the same room—as if there was light shining through everything. Everything became luminous, and it was radiant but soft all at the same time. I also experienced a kind of falling away of the sharp boundaries between the self and the world that mark our ordinary, everyday consciousness. These experiences were accompanied by amazement and wonder and a sense that I was seeing more clearly than I'd ever seen in my life. They were also full of joy; I could have lived in that state of consciousness forever. I would never have gotten old. Then I realized that those we call the mystics of all religions call these experiences, such as I had, experiences of God or the sacred. Suddenly the word God *referred to something that was manifestly real. I've never doubted the reality of God ever since those experiences.*

Group Response to the Teaching

What are your responses to hearing Borg speaking of these mystical times?

Have any of you had experiences you would term *mystical*?

What are the kind of experiences (not necessarily mystical) that bring you to the declaration that Borg makes: "I've never doubted the reality of God ever since."

Use the space below to make personal notes that complete this statement: "I experienced the sacred (the reality of God) when..."

OPTION 5: GOD DISCLOSED IN A LIFETIME

Beginning Conversation

In the space below draw your life's timeline; mark personal stages of spiritual awareness, religious activity, and awareness of God. Note the people or experiences that had an impact on your personal journey of spiritual and religious formation. Share these in pairs or triads.

The Teaching

Borg makes reference to his own theological growth from childhood, through his 20s and 30s up to the present time, as do a number of the other group members on the DVD. What insights do you take from all that has been shared both on the DVD and also in your group? Note insights below that you want to remember.

Group Response to the Teaching

Implied in this attention to life stages is the understanding that we are never finished. We are indeed evolutionary beings who carry an awareness of the "unfolding" nature of our lives. Think about where you are on your spiritual path today:

- What challenges and opportunities currently present themselves to you?
- What practices enable you to stay open to the movement of the Spirit?

OPTION 6: OUR NEED, GOD'S RESPONSE

Beginning Conversation

What do you need in your relationship with God today?

The Teaching

David, one of the participants in the group on the DVD, talks about his need for God in this way:

> *I want God to father me. I'm desperate for that. It's not as an authority figure. I want to be an apprentice. I want to become like father. I want to know, as a man, what masculinity is. I believe there is something that God is teaching me about that. I struggle with the idea of a personal God. Yet all the things I just said are all about the personal intimacy of experiences with God.*

Group Response to the Teaching

What is the impact on you of hearing David speak this way about his desire for relationship with God?

When have you spoken with God in the way David does?

What words would you use to express the quality of the relationship you want with God? For example, *accompanier, safe presence, energizer, holy guide*, etc. Use the space here to note words or phrases concerning that relationship:

OPTION 7: FINDING OUR GOD LANGUAGE

Beginning Conversation

When do you communicate with God? What form does that communication take?

The Teaching

In the DVD, Ashley, one of the participants, says the following:

> When I sit down to pray, instinctively my mind and heart still go to God "out there." After 20 years of trying to find God as something connected to me rather than separate from me, the rubber hits the road when I sit down to pray, and God is still someone I'm appealing to rather than communing with.

And Borg responds:

> When I pray, I address God as if God were a person. I talk to God as if God were right here. I regularly speak to God as Lord, or speak to God as if God is a person right here because I think my relationship to God is personal even though I don't think of God as a person. So for me the language of personification, by which I mean personifying God as if God were a person, is utterly natural. When I reflect back on my childhood, I think that what happened was that I began to literalize those personifications that then led to God as a person-like being separate from other beings. For me personal language in prayer and worship seems utterly natural.

Group Response to the Teaching

In the space below complete the statement below in as many ways as you can. After a period of time share these in the group.

When I pray I...

What insights about communication with God come from this conversation?

What new practices of communication with God might you try as a result of hearing these reflections? Note those in the space provided here.

Hymns are another form of scripted and spoken communication with God. Take time to thumb through your church's hymnbook for examples of hymns that allow you to experience a connection with the divine.

Borg quotes the poem by Denise Levertov, "The Avowal." You are invited to use it as part of your closing for this session.

> As swimmers dare
> to lie face up to the sky
> and water bears them,
> as hawks rest upon air
> and air sustains them,
> so would I learn to attain
> freefall, and float
> into Creator Spirit's deep embrace,
> knowing no effort earns
> that all-surrounding grace.

"THE AVOWAL" BY DENISE LEVERTOV, FROM OBLIQUE PRAYERS, COPYRIGHT ©1984 BY DENISE LEVERTOV. REPRINTED BY PERMISSION OF NEW DIRECTIONS PUBLISHING CORP.

SESSION | 2

JESUS

BEFORE THE SESSION

Many people like to come to these times of group conversation having given consideration on their own to some of the issues that will be raised. We intend these five reflective questions to open in your mind, memory and emotions some aspects of the topic for this session. Note your reflections in the space provided here.

Why does Jesus matter to you (if he does)?

What does Easter mean to you?

What does it mean to you to respond wholeheartedly to Jesus' call to "Follow me"?

What difference does it make to you that Jesus was a faithful practicing Jew?

How has relationship with the post-Easter Jesus changed your life?

OPTION 1: WHY JESUS MATTERS TO CHRISTIANS

Beginning Conversation
Why does Jesus matter to you? Go ahead; be honest. If the answer is, "He doesn't yet," then say that. If the answer is, "Years ago he used to, but I don't know that he does anymore," go with that. And if the answer is, "He shapes my whole life," say that as confidently as you feel it.

Take time in the group to hear all the ways that Jesus matters to each of you. Use the space below to note responses of other group members that you want to remember.

The Teaching
Later on the DVD you will hear Marcus Borg make this opening statement:

> *Jesus matters greatly for Christians. From the beginning of Christianity, Jesus has been the decisive revelation, disclosure or epiphany of what can be seen of God in a human life.*

Group Response to the Teaching
What is it that Jesus specifically discloses to you about the character and passion of God?

More Teaching
On the DVD Borg also makes this statement:

> *There are two primary sources for Christians: the Bible and Jesus. Orthodox and traditional Christianity has always placed greater authority in Jesus than in the Bible, or, we might say, "the word become person (Jesus) trumps the word become words (Bible)."*

More Group Response
Talk together about this idea that Borg puts forward of "Jesus trumping the Bible." When were times when you've had a sense of the person of Jesus carrying more weight than the Bible?

OPTION 2: KNOWING THE PRE-EASTER AND POST-EASTER JESUS

Beginning Conversation

Talk together about the various ways that you, as a person of faith, have used these two words: *Jesus* and *Christ*.

The Teaching

Play the initial 9.5 minutes of the DVD in which Marcus Borg speaks about two different realities represented by the word *Jesus*. A summary follows.

The name Jesus refers to two different realities:

- The pre-Easter Jesus…
  — was a flesh and blood (probably about 110 lb., 5'1") 1st-century Galilean Jew.
  — grew up as a peasant in a village and was executed by the Romans around the year 30.
  — is dead and gone, not brought back to life.
  — was not different in kind from us.
  — was an utterly remarkable human being.
  — was a Jewish mystic who experienced and knew God (didn't just believe in God).
  — was a healer and wisdom teacher who taught a way and a path.
  — was a prophet who announced the coming of the Kingdom of God and challenged the domination system of his time.
  — was so open to the Spirit of God that he could be filled with that Spirit.
  — discloses what can be seen of God in a human life.

- The post-Easter Jesus…
  — is what Jesus became in Christian experience and in Christian thought, language and tradition after his death.
  — is the risen Christ who is one with God and has all the qualities of God.
  — is a spiritual reality that can be experienced anywhere.
  — is one of the names of God.
  — is an expression of what the followers of Jesus, even to this day, continued to experience and know of him after his death (the truth of Easter).
  — is an experience of the risen Christ.
  — is God seen in the face of Jesus.

Group Response to the Teaching

Move into pairs and imagine that the person you are with has never heard of this distinction between the two ways of speaking of Jesus. Without reference to the notes, explain to them as clearly as you can this key understanding of the different meanings of the word *Jesus*.

More Teaching

Borg is careful to issue this warning about the distinction:

> *When we project qualities of the post-Easter Jesus back onto the pre-Easter Jesus, we make the pre-Easter Jesus not one of us.*

More Group Response

When have you been aware of this projection happening?

Why is it so important that we see Jesus as "one of us"?

OPTION 3: FINDING THE COURAGE TO FOLLOW

Beginning Conversation

Imagine that your response to the call of Jesus to "follow me" could be measured on a scale from 0 to 100. How would you determine where to place yourself? Note your response here:

How big is the gap between where you see yourself and where you'd like to be? Discuss this with your group.

The Teaching

Play the next 14 minutes of the DVD, stopping after Erica says, "what was he trying to disclose and bring to people, bring to humanity, that wasn't here before?" This section includes the reflections of the group members who were meeting with Borg. They address almost exclusively the matter of what it takes to give oneself to the way of Jesus and what keeps one from doing that. In the course of their conversation, Mike, one of the group members, makes reference to an imaginary scale of measurement: "actually following Jesus"—5%, "wanting the passion to follow Jesus"—95%. Watch this segment now.

Group Response to the Teaching

As you listen to the five participants in the group with Borg, note where you find them speaking in a way that connects with your own experience and feelings. Share those places of connection with the others in your group.

OPTION 4: JESUS' WAY: PERSONAL AND GLOBAL TRANSFORMATION

Beginning Conversation

Lyn, one of the participants in the DVD group, says the following:

> *As we deepen our personal transformation and lower our defenses, this allows us to love more. Then the desire for justice and the desire to be involved deepens to a greater level. From the other side, I would think that being involved in social justice issues would open our hearts so that we would want to develop the personal transformation. I would think that it would transform us as human beings. It feels like the potential is circular.*

Where and when have you experienced this circular interplay that Lyn names:
- intentional personal growth leading to action, and
- involvement in global and social change resulting in personal transformation?

Note those situations for yourself in the space provided and then share as you are ready:

The Teaching

You have already heard Marcus Borg speaking about the two key aspects of the message of the pre-Easter Jesus:
- The Way…
  — is a path to be followed.
  — is the way of life—of centering ever more deeply in God.
  — is the way he knew as a Jewish mystic.
  — is the path of personal transformation.
- The Kingdom (Jesus' passion)…
  — is God's dream for the earth which is for justice—economic, nonviolent and peaceful.
  — is about the transformation of the world.

Group Response to the Teaching

In each of the spaces below make notes on two things:

- the way these are already part of your faith and spiritual practice
- notes to yourself about how you could deepen both aspects of your life

Share your reflections and intentions as you are ready.

The Way of Personal Transformation

Bringing About God's Dream for the Earth

OPTION 5: HOW A JEWISH MYSTIC BECAME A CHRISTIAN LORD

Beginning Conversation

Erica, one of the participants in the Borg group, speaks about her quest to know more about the Jewish roots of Christianity. Note your own questions about the origins of the one called *Jesus*. These may not be answered in this session, but sharing them openly with one another builds relationship and raises the possibility that someone else in the group may have a response for you, or even a better question!

The Teaching

Watch the final 3 minutes of the DVD, in which Marcus Borg says the following:

It's utterly crucial for Christians to recognize how deeply Jewish Jesus was. A shorthand way of expressing that might be to say "from Jewish mystic (Jesus) to Christian Lord, (his status for Christians)." Then if we go on to puzzle about how a Jewish mystic became the central figure of a religion that is primarily gentile, meaning non-Jewish, I think the explanations are historical circumstance. There are two factors worth mentioning.

First, the message of Jesus was initially open to marginalized people within Judaism, people who in terms of the standards of convention and the standards of the culture were virtually outcasts and, in some cases, outcasts and untouchables. Within a decade of the death of Jesus, some of his followers began to include gentiles (non-Jews) within the early Christian movements on the grounds that if these marginalized and untouchable people within Judaism can be

part of this Jesus movement, then why not gentiles. The more that early Christianity included gentiles, the more it seemed to other Jews not to be a Jewish movement.

So it was the extension of Jesus' own activity from the marginalized within Judaism to the gentiles that eventually led to the parting of the ways between these two traditions. And it took time. A number of scholars think that as late as the year 250 that maybe at least half of Christians were still Jewish and that it's really in the 300s and afterwards, when Christianity became the official religion of the Roman Empire, that it became an overwhelmingly gentile religion. The process of separation and distinction was gradual and it had to do with historical circumstances and not that Jesus himself imagined a worldwide religion that would embrace both Jew and gentile. He saw himself as doing something within Judaism, which doesn't mean that gentile Christianity is a mistake. It's just not what he had in mind.

Group Response to the Teaching

What information in these three paragraphs is new to you? How does it change your perspective on...

- Jesus' intentions in his ministry?
- the early history of the Christian movement?
- the influence of the Roman Empire in Christian and Jewish history?
- Christian relationships with Judaism in the last two millennia?

OPTION 6: CLOSING

In this whole session, the study hasn't made reference to specific places in the gospel narrative of Jesus' life, to what he said and did. However, it's quite likely that some of those moments in his life and ministry came to mind as you watched, discussed and reflected. In this time of closing go around the circle and, without making comment, just complete this statement in a way that feels right for you:

I'm thinking about the moment when Jesus...

After these have been shared, say the prayer of Jesus, beginning *Our Father and Mother God who art in heaven...*

SESSION | 3

SALVATION

BEFORE THE SESSION

Many people like to come to these times of group conversation having given consideration on their own to some of the issues that will be raised. We intend these five reflective questions to open in your mind, memory and emotions some aspects of the topic for this session. Note your reflections in the space provided here.

What words, images, memories and experiences do you associate with the word *salvation*?

Sin is another problematic word for many. What is your current understanding of this word? How has that changed from earlier years?

What influential forces shaped the way you see God, afterlife, salvation, sin and faith today?

When were the times in your life that you would say, in the words of Psalm 23, that you were in "the darkest valley"? What made it possible for you to move beyond that time? If you are still in that time, in what ways do you feel accompanied?

What images, symbols, words, rituals and practices support you on the way?

OPTION 1: GETTING RID OF "SALVATION" BAGGAGE

Beginning Conversation

Brainstorm together all the words and images that you associate with the word *salvation*. What feelings do you have about this word? What memories and experiences come with it?

The Teaching

 Play the whole of the DVD segment for this session.

Concerning the word *salvation,* Marcus Borg says, "It's one of those loaded words, and yet it is utterly central to the Christian vocabulary."

Borg presents us with two contrasting ways of understanding salvation:

Sin-based	Transformation-focused
• Emphasizes the afterlife. • To be saved means being confident that your actions and beliefs have prepared you for heaven. • Salvation equals being saved from your sins. • Jesus is savior, the one who died because of our sins and in our place (atonement). • Jesus' death makes it possible for us to go to heaven. • Distorts what being Christian means.	• Focuses on what happens this side of death. • Salvation in the Bible is never about the afterlife. • Does *not* emphasize our sinfulness. • New Testament writers did not see the story of Jesus as being primarily about the afterlife. • The message of the New Testament is about transformation of self and world in this life, not preparation for the next.

Ashley, one of the Participants in Borg's group says:

> In my growing up I was constantly reminded of my original sin, my brokenness, with the result that there was shame around things like body and sensuality. The notion that salvation is available to me now is so powerful and yet there is this wall between me and that grace. That wall is made up of things like culture, family history, personal history, psychology, brain chemistry and education. Ultimately there is this choice that needs to be made. That's what's so profound about this notion that resurrection of my life is possible now. It's up to me to seize the opportunity! It's not something I have to wait another 50 years for until I die.

Borg:

> And, of course, the paradoxical thing about it is that it is up to you, but you can't get it just by grabbing. And so in some ways it's also about getting out of the way—whatever that means.

Group Response to the Teaching

Many people have had the same experience as Marcus and Ashley: experiencing a sin-based understanding of the way of Jesus and then being liberated into a transformational understanding. In the group, take time to share your experiences of these two different paths. As Ashley said, it's not easy to leave sin and salvation theology behind. It's like a wall that takes a long time to pull down. What experience do you have of this wall?

If you have dealt with something like the wall yourself, what made it possible to deal with that wall? At the end of the discussion talk about fresh insights you will take from it.

OPTION 2: THE PATH OF TRANSFORMATION

Beginning Conversation

Think of a time in your life that was troubling or problematic for you in some way. What word(s) would you use to describe that time?

What did it take to move you out of that trouble to a better time?

The Teaching

Marcus Borg talks about this journey of transformation in this way:

> The Bible has multiple images and metaphors for the human condition, the human predicament, the human problem, from which we need deliverance. Each of these ways of describing the problem points to a certain kind of solution as well. A central image: our problem is that we are in bondage. This is the heart of the Exodus story. It's also the heart of the New Testament perception of our being in bondage to the principalities and powers, that is, structures of evil that rule the world. If our problem is bondage then the solution is not forgiveness, but it's liberation. Or, we can be in bondage to the Pharaoh inside our heads—that psychological mechanism inside our minds that demands that we justify ourselves—that we measure up. That's an internal bondage to which the solution is liberation.
>
> The Bible frequently speaks of us as being blind; there are "those who have eyes and do not see." If the problem is blindness, then the solution is gaining our sight, seeing again.
>
> Another image: if the problem is a sense of separation, even alienation, then the need is to reconnect, and the means for doing that is a journey of reconnection, a journey of return. That's the biblical image of exile and return.
>
> Just one more: the Bible speaks of us being dead in the midst of life. ([Recall] that great saying of Jesus when he says about living people, "Leave the dead to bury the dead.") If you're alive and yet dead then obviously the solution is resurrection or rebirth. My point is that all of these are images of salvation in the Bible, and all of them are about transformation this side of death.

Group Response to the Teaching

The Human Condition	What We Need for Transformation	Times When This Dynamic of Transformation Has Been Real in My Own Life
Bondage, captivity	liberation	
blindness	sight, to be able to see clearly	
separation, alienation, exile	reconnection, return	
being dead in the midst of life	resurrection, rebirth	

Fill in the final column of this chart. When everyone has finished, share these personal examples with one another. What similarities are there in your journeys of transformation?

OPTION 3: THE MYSTERY OF TRANSFORMATION

Beginning Conversation

Option 2 led us into a reflection on the themes of transformation, but what is it that sets the transformation in motion?

As you think about times of significant change in your own life, what instigated the transformation?

The Teaching

Lyn, one of the participants in the Borg group, says the following:

> I keep being surprised—over and over and over—at how many layers there are to that process of transformation, and how much the blinders can be on. It happens all the time for me! It's like, "How did I not see that? How did I not get that?" You can't make yourself see things that you don't see. It almost takes somebody else to bump up against you in some way...or your read something...or sometimes it just comes. I don't fully understand how that process unfolds. There's a mystery about it.

And later she observes:

> I think it has to occur in groups—that connection—or in twos. We can't do it by ourselves or get to it in our own heads. It takes somebody else to reflect, or somebody else to give you feedback, or somebody else to make a comment or connect some piece of themselves. It's hard to find in a way that's safe, that place where we help each other knock the walls down or just walk alongside.

Group Response to the Teaching

Where does your own experience connect with Lyn's?

When have you felt as though something mysterious and unnamable was at work in your life, transforming what might have seemed unchangeably frozen? Make notes and then share with one other person or the whole group.

OPTION 4: CLOSING WITH IMAGES AND METAPHORS OF GRACE

Ashley, one of the participants in the Borg group, offers a metaphor as a way of thinking about the positive process of transformation:

> I used to live in south Oregon. Part of the time I lived down in the valley, and the rest of the time I lived at 2500 feet. In the winter there would be inversions, and the fog would roll into the valley, and it was just so dark during the day—overcast, impenetrable fog. All you had to do was drive up to the cabin where I was living and it was light, sunshine and glorious beauty above the fog. I think about that in my life all the time. God is just right there; there's just this cloud layer that's separating me from God or Spirit—or whatever it is that would be that life-giving force.

Take time to write quickly—without too much thought—words and images that speak to you of the grace, possibility and power of transformation. Use the space here.

After having time to note some of these words and images, go around the circle and share them, one image at a time (you might have several rounds of sharing).

Use this version of Psalm 23 in closing.

> O my Beloved, you are my shepherd,
>   I shall not want;
> You bring me to green pastures for
>   rest
> and lead me beside still waters
>   renewing my spirit.
> You restore my soul.
> You lead me in the path of goodness
>   to follow Love's way.
> Even though I walk through the
> valley of the shadow and of death,
>   I am not afraid;
> For You are ever with me;
>   your rod and your staff they
>   guide me,
>   they give me strength and
>   comfort.
> You prepare a table before me
> in the presence of all my fears;
>   you bless me with oil,
>   my cup overflows.
> Surely goodness and mercy will
>   follow me
>   all the days of my life;
> and I shall dwell in the heart of the
>   Beloved forever.

SESSION | 4

PRACTICE

BEFORE THE SESSION

Many people like to come to these times of group conversation having given consideration on their own to some of the issues that will be raised. We intend these five reflective questions to open in your mind, memory and emotions some aspects of the topic for this session. Note your reflections in the space provided here.

What are some of the spiritual or religious practices you follow in your life today?

As you think of your life as a spiritual or religious path, what were some of the features of the way on which you have walked?

What is your practice of prayer?

What were some of the truly memorable moments of worship in your life? What contributed to making them so significant in your journey of Spirit and faith?

For what are you grateful?

As we begin this session on practice, it's appropriate that we actually experience a practice that helps the group open well. Someone from your group will read the words of instruction that follow, pausing after each statement, while remaining members engage in the practice.

This is a practice of intention:

- Set aside whatever you are holding, and stand behind your chair.
- Take a moment to feel grounded and centered as you stand here.
- As you arrive here for this session, you come from all the other matters that occupy your life.
- Right now, you want to be as present as you can be to the life of this group and the process of learning.
- Notice the distractions that might keep you from being fully present here: anxieties and fear, unfinished conversations, unresolved feelings, moments of happiness and celebration, unfolding plans, urgencies from other places, and so on.
- On the outside of the circle, leave whatever would keep you from being present in this session.
- There may be things that you will need to reconnect with when the session is over, but for now you can set them aside and be present here.
- When you feel ready to be present with intention to this circle of learners, move into the circle and take your seat.
- Now we'll go around the circle and say our names in this way: "My name is _____, and I am here."

OPTION 2: ALL THAT WE MEAN BY PRACTICE

Beginning Conversation

What comes to mind from your own life when you hear the word *practice*?

What are some of your current practices?

Talk in the group about the way these practices are real for you today. Use the space below to note practices that emerge from the conversation that you might want to consider for your own practiced life.

The Teaching

Play the DVD and hear definitions and examples of practice offered by Marcus Borg and his friends.

Group Response to the Teaching

As you listened to the DVD, what was new for you about the meaning of practice?

What ideas appealed to you as opportunities for shaping your own spiritual and faith life?

Share your initial responses to the DVD in the group.

OPTION 3: THE WAY OF JESUS

Beginning Conversation
At what times in your life have you most sensed that the Christian life is about a path to follow rather than a set of beliefs to which you must adhere?

What difference did it make for you to see discipleship as a path?

The Teaching
Marcus Borg says:

> *The earliest post-Easter name for the followers of Jesus according to the book of Acts (9:1-2), was* Followers of the Way. *To think of Christianity as a way or a path is very helpful, in part because many Christians think of being Christian as being primarily about a set of beliefs, but originally it was a way or a path to follow. Practices are the practical means by which we embark upon that path of transformation that is following Jesus.*

Group Response to the Teaching
In order to think clearly and creatively about the Way of Jesus as a path on which you walk, imagine 10 steps on that path that represent a practice to follow. These may be practices you already follow or ones that you are aware of but have not yet begun. This is not about making a commitment to these practices; it's only a way to begin to imagine what a path of practice might look like. Feel free to draw on the ideas that already mentioned on the DVD.

Fill in the ten steps now. When everyone is ready, share any insights that come from imagining the path.

OPTION 4: PRAYER AS PRACTICE

Beginning Conversation

When do you find yourself in prayer? If you have a practice of prayer, what difference does it make in your daily living?

The Teaching

These statements about prayer are all made on the DVD:

- Prayer is about paying attention to my relationship with God.
- When I was a child, prayer consisted more of asking for things. Now, as an adult, it's more about paying attention.
- The fault of the disciples in the Garden of Gethsemane is that they fell asleep when Jesus had asked them to prayerfully pay attention.
- I find it much easier to stay focused on contemplative prayer when I'm praying in a group.
- There's a collective energy that is palpable when I pray in a group.
- Centering prayer—the prayer of internal silence as distinct from verbal prayer—is attracting many people in North America.
- If we can connect with the divine through the ordinary things, which make up most of our living, then more of our life will be connected to God.
- Prayer transforms those who pray.

Group Response to the Teaching

Put a check mark beside the statements above that you might have made had you been asked. What other statements would you make about what prayer means to you? Record those in the space in the next column, and then share them with one another.

Other statements about prayer:

1.

2.

3.

4.

5.

OPTION 5: WORSHIP AS PRACTICE

Beginning Conversation

Share with one another some of the special worship times in your life. What was it that made them so memorable?

What are some of the worshipful moments you have in common?

The Teaching

In the DVD you heard Borg say that we praise God, not because God requires it, but because it is good for us. Worship *forms* and *informs* us as we open ourselves to the reality and presence of God.

Group Response to the Teaching

What are the ways that you have been formed and informed by worship? In the chart below make note of some of these aspects of your religious formation. Two are given as examples.

The Action of Worship	The Way It Forms Me/Us
When I/we... sing hymns in community...	...I am vulnerable and broken open; able to feel and hear less defensively.
When I/we... hear prayers of gratitude and concern for God's world...	...my heart opens, and I feel more empowered to respond with action.
When I/we...	
When I/we...	
When I/we...	
When I/we...	
When I/we...	
When I/we...	

In what ways might you be more intentional
in your choices concerning worship: the kind
of worship opportunities you might look for,
the frequency with which you worship, the
unhelpful and irritating aspects of worship
you might choose to avoid or change, the
alternative kinds of worship you might
encourage or plan, and the redress of balance
you might initiate in your worship life?

OPTION 6: CLOSING IN GRATITUDE

Before the session gather two small bowls, one holding dried beans, shells and/or small stones.

Karen, one of the participants in Borg's group, describes her practice of gratitude:

> *I have gratitude bowls at home and at work which I keep on my desk. They are filled with beans and rocks and shells. When I go in to start my day at work, I light a candle and move a bean from one bowl to the other, thinking of something for which I'm grateful. I try to move as many beans and shells and rocks from bowl to bowl over the course of the day. This gratitude practice cultivates my heart opening. By doing that I am in more conscious alignment with the divine. The practice changes me. It puts me in touch with my soul's intention for my daily life.*

Take time to go around the circle with each person moving beans, shells or rocks from one bowl to the other and naming something for each object that you each give thanks, both in the life of your group and in your life beyond the group.

SESSION | 5

COMMUNITY

BEFORE THE SESSION

Many people like to come to these times of group conversation having given consideration on their own to some of the issues that will be raised. We intend these five reflective questions to open in your mind, memory and emotions some aspects of the topic for this session. Note your reflections in the space provided here.

What are your memorable experiences of faith-focused or Spirit-centered community? What made these experiences so special?

What communities in the Bible stand out for you? What qualities make those particular communities memorable?

Where and how do you experience Christian community today?

What are you looking for that community might offer at this time in your life?

What appreciations do you have for the members of this small group community with whom you have been meeting for five weeks?

OPTION 1: OPENING INTO COMMUNITY

As you come together in community take a moment to acknowledge each member of the group by going around the circle, naming and welcoming each person by saying: "*(Name)*, in the name of Christ, we welcome you!"

OPTION 2: STORIES OF COMMUNITY

Beginning

What are your memorable experiences of faith-focused or Spirit-centred community?

What was it that made these events so special? Share these memories with one another.

The Teaching

Play the DVD, noting especially the stories of community recounted by Borg and his friends.

Group Response to the Teaching

From your own stories and from the stories you just heard on the DVD, identify the following three things. Space is provided for your notes and reflections.

Some factors that tend to deepen the experience of community:

The influence that positive experiences of community can have on a person's formation:

What it is that makes us yearn for community:

OPTION 3: COMMUNITIES OF THE BIBLE

Beginning

What communities in the Bible stand out for you?

What qualities make those particular communities memorable? Note some examples as people share them.

The Teaching

Marcus Borg makes these points in his references to Biblical communities:

- Community and not individual spirituality is central to our Judeo-Christian tradition.
- The story of Israel in the Hebrew Scriptures is more about the community's relationship with God than about individual relationship with God.
- This tradition is also about life with one another in community, including the establishment of civil and criminal law, which are all part of the covenant with God.

- In the Christian Scriptures Paul uses the expression *In Christ* with great frequency as the central image for life in a community that is centred in Christ.
- These communities to which Paul refers were small and intimate, meeting in spaces where only 10-15 people could gather.
- Paul uses the language of new family (*my brothers and sisters*), not only as a term of affection but also as a way of emphasizing that the intimacy within these Christ communities was of the same kind and involved the same obligations as those of biological siblings.
- The mutual sharing of food marked these Spirit-centered communities.

Group Response to the Teaching

These biblical communities emerged in very specific historical and cultural situations. For example, Borg points out that at the time of Paul, cities were settled by immigrants from the countryside who were forced into the cities where death rates were high and the structure of the traditional family was destroyed. Regardless of the reasons for the centrality of community in our tradition, this emphasis on community is real.

In what ways do you see your faith community following that tradition?

In what ways might you deepen that connection between your faith community and the biblical traditions of community?

OPTION 4: CHRISTIAN COMMUNITY TODAY

Beginning

Where and how do you experience Christian community today?

What characteristics mark it as being "in Christ" or Christian?

The Teaching

On the DVD you heard Borg identify three things as purposes of Christian community today:

- Christian community is about *worship* (which we focused on in the last session on practice).
- Christian community is about *formation*.
  - We are socialized (re-formed) into a Christian vision of life while still being immersed in a culture that is radically different from the biblical vision of the way things should be.
  - Formation happens through such things as Christian education, knowing our story and worship.
- Christian community is about *faithfulness* to God.
  - Faithfulness means participating in God's passion which is the well being of the world.

— Christian community responds to God's passion through such things as political engagement, ecological initiative, partnership with all creation and individual ethical acts sustained by participation in community.

Group Response to the Teaching

In his teaching Borg presents three distinct ways of evaluating the focus and effectiveness of our faith communities. In the last session we addressed the ways that worship forms us individually and communally, so in this session we will focus on the other two expressions of community.

Fill out the four quadrants below as indicated. When finished, share your reflections with one or two other people.

Return to the group and share any insights you have about how well your faith community lives out its call to faith formation and to faithfulness in pursuing God's passion for all creation. What new opportunities call you as a community?

	What my faith community offers me	What I contribute to my faith community
Formation into the Christian Vision of Life		
Faithfulness in Pursuing God's Passion		

OPTION 5: THE YEARNING FOR COMMUNITY

Beginning

What are you looking for that community might offer at this time in your life?

The Teaching

In his opening remarks Borg says:

> The United States is probably the most individualistic culture in the history of the world, so we don't typically think in communitarian terms.

Not surprisingly then, several of the participants in the group meeting with Borg spoke of their own yearning for community. Here are just two of those statements:

Lyn:

> I grew up in a small town in a very large extended family where everyone knew everything about everybody. When I was just out of college I couldn't wait to get away from all that! Now the longing is for that again: for that connecting, community, extended family, church and God.

Karen:

> I love that image of the early church—before it was the church—just a small gathering. That's what I desire in my spiritual community: to have small study groups and opportunities to study in more depth and be more vulnerable and more authentic. And then to have opportunities for community to grow out of that and reach back to the larger congregation.

Borg has also said this:

> There is an enormous opportunity for the church to speak of itself as a place of community because community is almost gone in our country.

Group Response to the Teaching

What can you say about your own yearning for community?

Do you have trouble finding enough community?

What does it take to find the community your heart desires?

If the community landscape is as bleak as Borg suggests, how might churches respond visibly to the desire for spiritually-based community?

OPTION 6: CLOSING THE COMMUNITY

This is the last of the five sessions. Make notes
as follows:

Significant Personal Learning From The Five Sessions
Things That Contributed To My Learning
My Appreciations For The Community

Take time to share one or two items from this
evaluation with the group.

Take time to hear anything else that needs to
be shared, so that no one takes away things that
really need to be said in the group.

Isaiah Blessing
(based on Isaiah 43:1-3a)

Take turns standing in the center of the group and receiving this spoken blessing from the other group members as each reaches out with one open hand. If the person being blessed wishes it, your hands can touch them. Insert the name of each person in the three spaces.

But now thus says God who created you, *(Name)*,

God who formed you, *(Name)*,

Do not fear, for I have called you by name, *(Name)*, you are mine.

When you pass through the waters, I will be with you;

and through the rivers, they shall not overwhelm you;

when you walk through fire you shall not be burned,

and the flames shall not consume you.

For I am your God.